UNIT

STRESS MANAGEMENT AND SELF-ESTEEM ACTIVITIES

PATRICIA RIZZO TONER

Just for the HEALTH of It!
Health Curriculum Activities Library

**THE CENTER FOR APPLIED
RESEARCH IN EDUCATION**
West Nyack, New York 10995

10 9 8 7 6 5 4 3 2

Library of Congress Cataloging-in-Publication Data

Toner, Patricia Rizzo, 1952-
    Stress-management and self-esteem activities / Patricia Rizzo Toner.
        p.   cm.—(Just for the health of it! ; unit 5)
    "Includes 90 ready-to-use activities and worksheets for grades
7-12."
    ISBN 0-87628-874-3
    1. Stress management for teenagers. 2. Self-esteem in
adolescence. 3. Activity programs in education. I. Title.
II. Series.
RA785.T65   1993
155.9′042′0835—dc20   93-14841
                                                                CIP

ISBN 0-87628-874-3 NB2I

**The Center for Applied Research
in Education,** Professional Publishing
West Nyack, New York 10995
Simon & Schuster, A Paramount Communications Company

Printed in the United States of America

DEDICATION

To my fellow field hockey coaches,

Lynn Ely, Terry Brookshaw, Sheila Murphy, Linda Pellegrino,
Marianne Paparone, Barb Clipsham, Sylvia Kalazs, Carol Morrow,
Joanne Stanton, and all those who deal with stress on a daily basis,
especially from August to November.

To the Council Rock field hockey players, past, present, and future,
who must deal with my stress on a daily basis.

Patricia R. Toner

ACKNOWLEDGMENTS

The source for many of the clip art images used in this resource is Presentation
Task Force which is a registered trademark of New Vision Technologies Inc.,
copyright 1991.

Thanks to Colleen Leh and Barb Snyder, Holland Junior High, Holland, Pennsylvania, for reviewing each activity and providing valuable feedback.

Thanks to Marianne Paparone, Amber, Pennsylvania for listening to me whine
about how much work I had to do.

ABOUT THE AUTHOR

Patricia Rizzo Toner, M.Ed., has taught Health and Physical Education in the
Council Rock School District, Holland, PA, for over 19 years, and she has also
coached gymnastics and field hockey. She is the co-author of three books: *What Are
We Doing in Gym Today?, You'll Never Guess What We Did in Gym Today!,* and
How to Survive Teaching Health. Besides her work as a teacher, Pat is also a
freelance cartoonist. A member of the American Alliance for Health, Physical
Education, Recreation and Dance, Pat received the Hammond Service Award, the
Marianna G. Packer Book Award and was named to *Who's Who Among Students in
American Colleges and Universities,* as well as *Who's Who in American Education.*

ABOUT <u>JUST FOR THE HEALTH OF IT!</u>

Just for the Health of It! was developed to give you, the health teacher, new ways to present difficult-to-teach subjects and to spark your students' interest in day-to-day health classes. It includes over 540 ready-to-use activities organized for your teaching convenience into six separate, self-contained units focusing on six major areas of health education.

Each unit provides ninety classroom-tested activities printed in a full-page format and ready to be photocopied as many times as needed for student use. Many of the activities are illustrated with cartoon figures to enliven the material and help inject a touch of humor into the health curriculum.

The following briefly describes each of the six units in the series:

Unit 1: *Consumer Health and Safety Activities* helps students recognize advertising techniques, compare various products and claims, understand consumer rights, distinguish between safe and dangerous items, become familiar with safety rules, and more.

Unit 2: *Diet and Nutrition Activities* focuses on basic concepts and skills such as the four food groups, caloric balance or imbalance, the safety of diets, food additives, and vitamin deficiency diseases.

Unit 3: *Relationships and Communication Activities* explores topics such as family relationships, sibling rivalry, how to make friends, split-level communications, assertiveness and aggressiveness, dating, divorce, and popularity.

Unit 4: *Sex Education Activities* teaches about the male and female reproductive systems, various methods of contraception ranging from abstinence to mechanical and chemical methods, sexually transmitted diseases, the immune system, pregnancy, fetal development, childbirth, and more.

Unit 5: *Stress-Management and Self-Esteem Activities* examines the causes and signs of stress and teaches ways of coping with it. Along with these, the unit focuses on various elements of building self-esteem such as appearance, values, self-concept, success and confidence, personality, and character traits.

Unit 6: *Substance Abuse Prevention Activities* deals with the use and abuse of tobacco, alcohol, and other drugs and examines habits ranging from occasional use to addiction. It also promotes alternatives to drug use by examining peer pressure situations, decision-making, and where to seek help.

To help you mix and match activities from the series with ease, all of the activities in each unit are designated with two letters to represent each resource as follows: Sex Education (SE), Substance Abuse Prevention (SA), Relationships and Communication (RC), Stress Management and Self-Esteem (SM), Diet and Nutrition (DN), and Consumer Health and Safety (CH).

About Unit 5

Stress-Management and Self-Esteem Activities, Unit 5 in *Just for the Health of It!*, gives you ninety ready-to-use activities to develop your students' awareness of the causes and effects of stress and factors that promote self-awareness and discovery. The activities include reproducibles to hand out to students, innovative games, puzzles and other techniques to enhance your presentations.

You can use these aids in any way you wish—to introduce a particular subject, to heighten student interest at a given point in a lesson, or to reinforce what students have already learned. Complete answer keys for the activity sheets are provided at the end of the unit. You may keep these for your own use or place a copy at some central location for student self checking.

For quick selection of appropriate activities, the table of contents provides general and specific topic heads and a complete listing of all worksheets and other activities in the unit. The ninety activities are organized into four main sections, including:

Stress. This section helps students understand stress and learn about ways to manage it through the use of more than fifteen reproducibles and activities grouped under three main heads:

- Stressors
- Signs and Symptoms of Stress
- Managing Stress

Reducing Stress. Two main topics in this section focus on practical ways to reduce stress:

- Goal Setting
- Time Management Strategies

Emotions. This section offers nearly twenty-five reproducibles and activities covering topics such as:

- Understanding Emotions
- Coping Strategies
- Mental Health Problems

Self Esteem. More than forty activities examine the following factors that contribute to self esteem:

- Strengths and Weaknesses
- Appearance and Self-Concept
- Values
- Success and Confidence
- Self-Discovery
- Personality

All of the reproducibles and activities in this unit are numbered consecutively and keyed to the unit with the letters **SM,** representing the Stress Management and Self-Esteem component of the series. These worksheets, games, puzzles, and activities can be put directly into your lessons.

I hope you'll enjoy using them as much as I do.

Patricia Rizzo Toner

CONTENTS

Personality

STRESS

- **Stressors**

- **Signs and Symptoms of Stress**

- **Managing Stress**

Name _____ **Date** _____

PHYSICAL CAUSES OF STRESS (SM-1)

DIRECTIONS: Near each picture is a physical factor that could lead to stress. In the spaces provided, list some things a person could do to eliminate that stressor from his or her life.

Misuse of Medication

_____
_____
_____
_____

Smoking

_____
_____
_____
_____

Poor Diet

_____
_____
_____

Lack of Exercise

_____
_____
_____
_____

Lack of Sleep

_____
_____
_____
_____

©1993 by The Center for Applied Research in Education

FAMILY STRESSORS (SM-2)

DIRECTIONS: Listed below are some factors that cause stress within a family. On the back of this sheet, write a paragraph for each factor explaining how you feel that stressor could affect a family.

Parents Fighting

Moving

Financial Problems

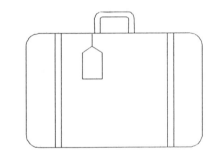

Family Member Leaving Home

Behavior Problems with Children

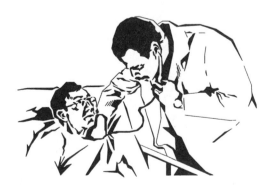

Health Problems in Family Members

Death of a Family Member

Name _____ **Date** _____

FAMILY STRESS LIST (SM-3)

DIRECTIONS: Interview your family members and ask what causes them stress. List the various stressors each person faces. Pick one person. What could YOU do to lessen one of their stressors?

MOM	DAD	SISTER(S)	BROTHER(S)	GRANDPARENTS	YOU

STRESS COMPARISON (SM-4)

DIRECTIONS: Each age group has its own stressors. What might be stress for one group, is not necessarily stress for another. In groups of three or four, brainstorm all the possible stressors people could face at each age. Compare your lists. Discuss which age group faces the most pressures and why.

1. INFANTS

2. CHILDREN

3. TEENAGERS

4. YOUNG ADULTS

5. PARENTS

6. ELDERLY PEOPLE

ENVIRONMENTAL STRESSORS (SM-5)

DIRECTIONS: As a society we face many pressures that can affect our lives. These stressors include forms of pollution, conflict between nations, natural disasters, and economic changes. Fill in the crossword puzzle below to show some of these stressors.

©1993 by The Center for Applied Research in Education

ACROSS

1. Armed conflict between nations.
5. Excessive environmental noise from planes, autos, industry, etc. (two words)
6. A violent, whirling wind accompanied by a funnel-shaped cloud.
7. A large quantity of water overflowing onto what is normally dry land.
9. A rise in prices brought about by an increase in the ratio of currency and credit to the goods available.

DOWN

2. Unhealthy elements in the air we breathe. (two words)
3. Unhealthy and impure water supply. (two words)
4. A chemical change accompanied by the emission of heat, light, and flames.
8. A cyclone with winds exceeding 73 m.p.h. and usually covering a large area.

Name _____ **Date** _____

JOB-RELATED STRESS (SM-6)

DIRECTIONS: In groups of three or four, brainstorm ways that a person could lessen the stress that he or she might feel from the factors listed below. Report your findings back to the class.

| **Starting a New Job** |

| **Retirement** |

| **Too Much Work** |

| **Possibility of Loss** |

| **Poor Relationships with Boss, Colleagues** |

| **Unclear Duties or Responsibilities** |

PUSH THE PANIC BUTTON (SM-7)

DIRECTIONS: We all have certain things or people that cause us to lose our composure from time to time. In this activity, try to figure out what causes YOU to "lose your cool." Once we begin to identify our stressors, we can learn to lessen their effect. Place a checkmark next to each factor that causes you stress. There are blank spaces provided so you can add your own.

What pushes your "stress buttons"?

_____ being late
_____ too much homework
_____ oral reports
_____ babysitting
_____ going to the dentist
_____ arguments with friends
_____ restrictions at home
_____ chores
_____ lack of sleep
_____ no date for a dance
_____ pimples
_____ physical education class
_____ math class
_____ English class
_____ health class
_____ social studies class
_____ other class_____
_____ cafeteria food
_____ nothing to do
_____ rude people
_____ no money
_____ no transportation
_____ playing on a sports team
_____ being cut from a sports team
_____ losing something valuable
_____ finding that a friend betrayed you
_____ parents fighting
_____ getting a detention or suspension

_____ your job
_____ taking tests
_____ video games
_____ using a computer
_____ closed-in spaces
_____ commercials
_____ interruptions while busy
_____ getting an injection
_____ arguments with parents
_____ fight with boyfriend/girlfriend
_____ losing
_____ careless drivers
_____ slow drivers
_____ loud people
_____ baby crying
_____ disrespectful children
_____ _____
_____ _____
_____ _____
_____ _____
_____ _____
_____ _____
_____ _____
_____ _____
_____ _____
_____ _____
_____ _____

THE COMFORT ZONE (SM-8)

We all have certain areas in which we feel confident or comfortable. Once we venture into unknown areas, we may feel vulnerable. This is known as "being out of the comfort zone." In the situations below, place a "+" if you would feel comfortable doing what is mentioned, a "0" if it would cause you to feel a little uncomfortable, or a "-" if it would take you out of your comfort zone.

WOULD YOU . . . .

_____ 1. introduce yourself to someone you never saw before?

_____ 2. apply for a job requiring an interview with the boss?

_____ 3. tell your boyfriend/girlfriend, in person, that you no longer want to see him/her?

_____ 4. tell your friend that he or she has body odor?

_____ 5. go on a date with someone that no one else likes?

_____ 6. refuse to do something that everyone else is doing?

_____ 7. refuse your only ride home if you suspected the driver was drunk?

_____ 8. make a speech in front of the student body?

_____ 9. go to a movie or restaurant by yourself?

_____ 10. stick up for a friend who everyone else is mad at?

_____ 11. run for class officer?

_____ 12. try out for a sports team?

_____ 13. go to a college hundreds of miles from home?

_____ 14. sit at a lunch table with people you didn't know, if no other seats were available?

_____ 15. start a conversation with a person you don't know?

ARE YOU A RISK-TAKER?

Name _____ Date _____

CHECK THIS OUT!! (SM-9)

DIRECTIONS: Look at the symptoms of stress listed below. Check *ALL* the symptoms that have applied or currently apply to you. Discuss your chart with a classmate. Are there any similarities? How much stress do you think you are currently under? Discuss ways that each of you could eliminate some of the stress that causes these problems.

Physical Symptoms

_____ headaches
_____ stomach aches
_____ dizziness
_____ back pain
_____ neck stiffness
_____ ulcer sores on
       tongue, mouth
_____ jaw pains
_____ constipation
_____ diarrhea
_____ weight loss
       or gain
_____ twitches
       (eyelids, face)
_____ weakness
_____ nausea
_____ indigestion
_____ overeating or
       loss of appetite
_____ skin problems
_____ cold hands or feet
_____ excessive sweating
_____ chest pains
_____ inability to sleep
_____ high blood pressure
_____ rapid or difficult
       breathing
_____ heart palpitations
_____ frequent urination
_____ heartburn
_____ excessive sleeping
_____ constant fatigue

Emotional Symptoms

_____ mood changes
_____ lack of
       concentration
_____ nightmares
_____ panic attacks
_____ anxiety
_____ withdrawing
       from others
_____ anger
_____ irritability
_____ crying
_____ thoughts of
       suicide
_____ depression
_____ confusion
_____ feelings of
       helplessness
_____ restlessness
_____ racing thoughts
_____ aggressiveness

Behavioral Symptoms

_____ smoking
_____ nail biting
_____ tapping
_____ pulling hair
_____ grinding teeth
_____ use of alcohol
_____ use of medication
_____ compulsive dieting
_____ compulsive overeating
_____ nervous laughter
_____ pacing
_____ lateness
_____ putting things off
_____ not caring about
       physical appearance

Name _____ **Date** _____

STRESSED OUT!! (SM-10)

DIRECTIONS: Unscramble the words and place them in the blanks to show the *PHYSICAL* signs and symptoms of stress. The letters in the circles will form a word that is a method of reducing stress. Write that hidden word in the blank at the bottom of the page.

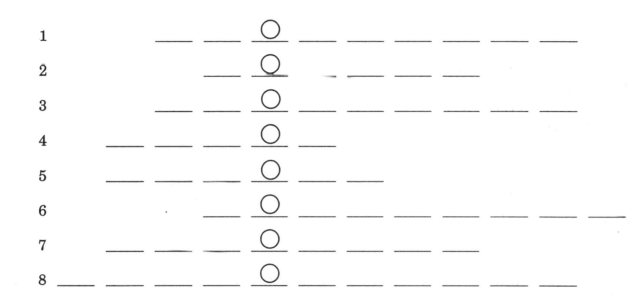

1. INCREASED <u>RBTEAHNGI</u> RATE

2. <u>XESSCE</u> SWEATING

3. CHANGES IN BLOOD <u>HCMEITRYS</u>

4. INCREASED <u>RTEHA</u> RATE

5. INCREASED <u>LESCMU</u> TENSION

6. DECREASED <u>GDISTOINE</u>

7. INCREASED BLOOD <u>EEPSRSUR</u>

8. DECREASED SKIN <u>RTAEPETMRUE</u>

HIDDEN WORD _____

HOW DO YOU SPELL RELIEF? (SM-11)

DIRECTIONS: Listed below are some examples of how people deal with stress. With a partner, brainstorm all the ways that people could deal with stress. Include both positive and negative methods. When you have compiled a list, go back and place an *X* in the boxes of the methods that are healthy ways to deal with stress.

☐ **smoking** _____   ☐ _____

☐ **drinking alcohol** _____   ☐ _____

☒ **exercise** _____   ☐ _____

☐ _____   ☐ _____

☐ _____   ☐ _____

☐ _____   ☐ _____

☐ _____   ☐ _____

☐ _____   ☐ _____

☐ _____   ☐ _____

☐ _____   ☐ _____

☐ _____   ☐ _____

Name _____   **Date** _____

STRESS JOURNAL (SM-12)

DIRECTIONS: To start managing stress, you must first recognize it. Fill in the stress journal entries twice in the morning, twice in the afternoon, and twice in the evening for two weeks. When the two weeks are over, discuss your observations with your classmates. What causes YOU the most stress? (Use as many sheets as necessary to complete the task.)

DATE	TIME	SITUATION	STRESS LEVEL	SIGNS
5/29	9:00am	(Where? With whom? Doing what?) At work... argued with boss.	(1–100) 85	Heart racing, headache, muscle tension

HAVE A LAUGH! (SM-13)

DIRECTIONS: One of the best stress relievers is laughter. Spending time with people who make you laugh is a good way to relax. Answer the questions below and have a laugh!

1. Who is one of the funniest people you know?

2. What is something this person said or did that made you laugh?

3. What is the funniest thing that has *ever* happened to you?

4. Do you like to tell jokes, hear jokes, or both?

5. Who is your favorite comedian?

6. What is your favorite comedy movie?

7. What is your favorite TV show? Is it a comedy?

8. What is your favorite TV commercial? Is it humorous?

9. Do you think you have a good sense of humor?

10. Did anything make you laugh today? If so, what?

©1993 by The Center for Applied Research in Education

©1993 by The Center for Applied Research in Education

Name _____ **Date** _____

HOW'S YOUR ATTITUDE? (SM-14)

DIRECTIONS: Take the quiz below to determine how your attitude affects your level of stress. Circle each number to indicate how strongly each statement makes you feel. Refer to the key to score your stress level.

	Strongly Agree	Agree Somewhat	Disagree Somewhat	Strongly Disagree
1. School is empty and has no meaning to me.	3	2	1	0
2. I feel satisfied with my schoolwork.	0	1	2	3
3. My life feels routine and boring.	3	2	1	0
4. I feel satisfied with my personal life.	0	1	2	3
5. There is not much new or exciting in my life.	3	2	1	0
6. My life has some specific purposes and goals.	0	1	2	3
7. My life does not meet my inner needs.	3	2	1	0
8. My life is taken up with burdens and responsibilities.	3	2	1	0
9. I believe there is a higher force or power guiding humanity.	0	1	2	3

SCORING

0–3   <u>Great</u>: You have a high level of effectiveness and creativity even under pressure.

4–7   <u>Balanced</u>: You have steady and effective performance in most situations.

8–12   <u>Feeling Some Strain</u>: You often feel overwhelmed or drained. You need some relief!

13 +   <u>Burned Out</u>: You have a great deal of difficulty and stress. It may impair your ability to function.

ATTITUDE ADJUSTMENT (SM-15)

DIRECTIONS: Listed below are some questions and suggestions for lessening stress by improving your attitude and outlook on life. Answer the questions honestly, then make an effort to follow the suggestions. You CAN improve your attitude!

1. What are the THREE most important needs you have in your life right now?

2. Are each of these needs being met? If not, which ones are not?

3. Name a strong belief that you have.

4. What action, if any, have you taken to emphasize that belief? What action or further action could you take?

5. What ONE thing could you do today to move toward meeting one of your life goals or needs? TRY TO DO SOMETHING EVERY DAY!

6. Imagine that you have only one year to live. What could you do in that year? (Be specific.) Why not do some of those things now?

7. Name the people for whom you are thankful. Tell someone you care today. (Send a card, call, visit, etc.)

8. Name the things for which you are grateful.

STRESS REDUCERS

- **Goal Setting**

- **Time Management**

ACTIVITY 1: DEAR BLABBY

Concept/ Description: Students will view problems from Dear Abby's columns but will not view her solutions or suggestions. The students will then devise their own solutions.

Objective: To have small groups of students brainstorm solutions to various problems, choose the best solution, and write an appropriate response.

Materials: Dear Abby columns dealing with teen concerns (remove, but save, Abby's responses)
Paper and pens or pencils

Directions:
1. Divide the class into small groups and distribute one or two Dear Abby columns to each group. (Be sure to separate Abby's responses.)
2. Have the groups read the problem, then brainstorm all the possible solutions. All brainstorm ideas should be written down.
3. Groups should then discuss the feasibility of the ideas and choose a solution to which all can agree.
4. Write the response as Abby might in her column.
5. Have the groups read their problems and solutions to the class.
6. Read Abby's actual answer and discuss.

Variations:
1. Have the students make up their own problems. Then distribute the problems to the groups as above.
2. Host a Dear Blabby panel discussion where three or four students will give their solutions as the "experts." The rest of the class can have problems that were previously written on cards to ask the panel.

Well...
I think that  the answer to your problem is...

Name _____ **Date** _____

GOAL SETTING (SM-16)

DIRECTIONS: Listed below are guidelines for setting goals. Answer the questions and try setting some reasonable goals for yourself. Goals are easier to accomplish when they are clear, specific, and broken down into steps you can manage.

GUIDELINES FOR SETTING GOALS

1. Understand Yourself

   What do you do well?
   What do you enjoy doing?
   What are the most important things in your life?

2. Make Clear, Specific Goals

   A goal should tell you exactly what you want and should be measurable. For example, "I want to score ten goals in lacrosse this season" is both clear and specific.

3. Goals Should Be Positive

   Say "I want to lose 5 pounds by Christmas" rather than "I don't want to be so fat."

4. Set Time Limits

   Give yourself a reasonable deadline in which to accomplish your goal.

5. Break Your Long Term Goals Down Into Smaller Parts

   If your ultimate goal is to be a professional basketball player, a realistic, specific short-term goal would be to make the varsity basketball team this year.

6. Write Your Goals Down

   Keeping your written goals where you can see them will help keep you focused on achieving them.

7. Check Your Progress

   Evaluate your progress towards your goals. Are you doing what needs to be done to meet your goals? If not, what can you do to get back on target?

TRY IT YOURSELF

Write three clear, specific, manageable goals for this coming week:

Write a one-page resume and mail it by 3:00 today.

1.

2.

3.

DO I MAKE MYSELF CLEAR? (SM-17)

DIRECTIONS: Listed below are some poorly defined goals. Some are not specific, some set no time constraints, some are unrealistic. Rewrite each goal to make it specific, clear, and manageable.

1. I want to do well in school this year.
   Ex. I want to get all *B*s this marking period.

2. I don't want to eat as much junk food.

3. I want to get along better with my little brother.

4. I want to be on the Olympic Diving Team.

5. I don't want to be so fat.

6. I want to get a nice car someday.

7. I want to get a job.

8. I want to wear better clothes.

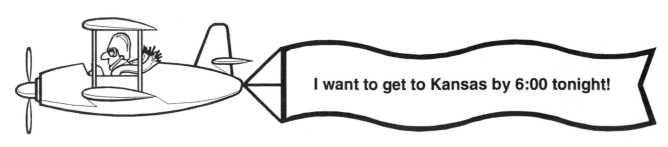

I want to get to Kansas by 6:00 tonight!

Name _____ **Date** _____

I'LL DO IT! (SM-18)

DIRECTIONS: Write down clear, specific goals that you can attain in the time spans listed. Be sure your goals are very specific.

Goals I will accomplish by:

tomorrow

1.
2.
3.

next weekend

1.
2.
3.

winter break

1.
2.
3.

the end of the school year

1.
2.
3.

the time I graduate from high school

1.
2.
3.

Pick any goal mentioned and list specific actions that you will take in order to achieve that goal:

1.
2.
3.
4.
5.

JUGGLE YOUR TIME (SM-19)

DIRECTIONS: Our time is divided into three categories: *self, school* or *career,* and *relation-ships*. The pie to the right shows a person who has a balanced lifestyle. In the circle provided, make a pie depicting your own lifestyle. Use the legend to color code your chart. Are you pleased with the time spent in each area? On the back of this sheet, explain how your time is spent for each category.

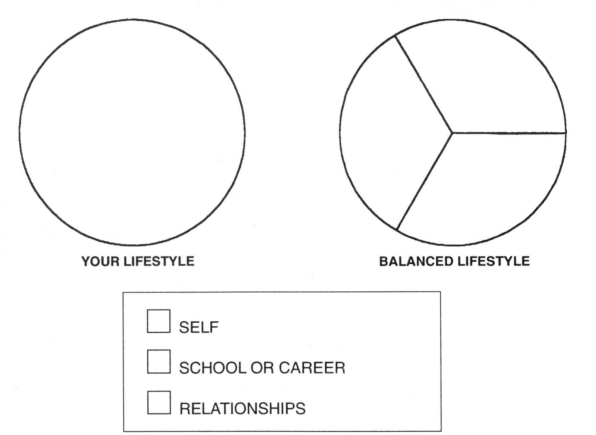

YOUR LIFESTYLE   **BALANCED LIFESTYLE**

☐ SELF

☐ SCHOOL OR CAREER

☐ RELATIONSHIPS

SELF: Time spent filling your personal needs such as sleep, fitness, spiritual needs, hobbies, sports, eating, etc.
SCHOOL OR CAREER: Time spent at work, in school, doing homework, maintaining a home, etc.
RELATIONSHIPS: Time spent with a mate, family, friends, in the community, etc.

FAMILY?   **JOB?**

FUN?   **HOUSE REPAIRS?**

Name _____ **Date** _____

TIME MANAGEMENT (SM-20)

DIRECTIONS: Full in the chart below in HOURS spent in each activity.
Be sure not to account for time more than once. For example,
don't count time spent eating lunch at school as eating time AND school time.
Compare the amount of free time you have with your classmates.

1. ## HOURS IN A WEEK: <u>168</u>

2. Sleeping Time: _____

3. Hours in School: _____

4. Hours in a Job: _____

5. Time Spent Doing Chores: _____

6. Eating Time: _____

7. Necessities (dressing, showering, doing hair, etc.): _____

8. Time in Extracurricular Activities (sports, band, chorus, etc.): _____

9. Transportation Time (to and from school, work, etc.): _____

10. Homework Time: _____

ADD lines 2 through 10: _____

SUBTRACT from line 1: _____

This number equals your FREE TIME: _____

Name _____ **Date** _____

TIME ON YOUR HANDS (SM-21)

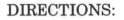

DIRECTIONS:

1. Pick a color to indicate used time and color in the Used Time box.
2. Pick a contrasting color to indicate free time and fill in the Free Time box.
3. On the left side of the chart fill in the hours of the day starting with the time you normally get up.
4. Color in the time blocks according to the colors you selected to indicate where you have free time during an average week. (Free time would be time NOT spent in school, asleep, eating, sports, working, etc.)

MON	TUES	WED	THURS	FRI	SAT	SUN

☐ FREE TIME   ☐ USED TIME

©1993 by The Center for Applied Research in Education

Name _____ **Date** _____

TIME MANAGEMENT STRATEGIES (SM-22)

DIRECTIONS: Listed below are some effective strategies for managing time and thereby reducing stress. Answer the questions and try the strategies. You CAN reduce stress in your life.

1. Write down your goals or the tasks you must complete for *this week*.

2. Make a priority list according to the importance of each task. Once you have written down each task, assign it a ranking as follows:

    1—MOST important
    2—LESS important
    3—LEAST important
    4—NOT important at all

    Do all of the tasks ranked 1, first. If you have a large number of top-ranked tasks, try this:

Priority list	Instructions
1. **write essay** ✓✓✓✓	Pick any five tasks and number them 1, 2, 3, 4, and 5.
2. **reading assignment**	Compare 1 to 2. Which is more important?
3. **clean room** ✓✓	Place a checkmark next to your decision.
4. **practice piano** ✓✓✓	Then compare 1 to 3, 1 to 4, 1 to 5, again placing checks next to the most important.
5. **organize dance** ✓	Continue comparing 2 to 3, 2 to 4, 2 to 5, 3 to 5, and 4 to 5.
	Which has the most checks? Do that task first!

3. Plan your schedule using a calendar or appointment book. Be sure to include all appointments, such as dentist, haircut, student council meetings, sports practices, and music lessons, in the proper time slots. Use the TO DO LIST worksheet (SM-23) as a handy tool to remind you of what you must do and when you must do it.

4. Do the most important tasks when you have the most energy. When do you have the most energy?

5. Eliminate all the unnecessary things you do that waste time. What do you do that wastes time?

6. Finish one thing before you start another. In other words, do what you are doing. Don't get sidetracked and start another task or project.

7. Write down everything. Keep a notepad and pencil with you and get in the habit of using it. Each time you are given an assignment or make an appointment, write it down, then add it to your TO DO LIST. Cross off each task when it is completed.

8. Ask for help, if you need it. If there are tasks that you don't have to do by yourself, ask other people for their help.

Name _____ **Date** _____

TO DO LIST (SM-23)

DIRECTIONS: List all of your appointments, meetings, assignments, practices, etc., on the chart below. Use it as a guide to help you manage your time. Cross off each item as you complete it.

MONDAY	
TUESDAY	
WEDNESDAY	
THURSDAY	
FRIDAY	
SATURDAY	
SUNDAY	

EMOTIONS

- **Understanding Emotions**

- **Coping Strategies**

- **Mental Health**

ACTIVITY 2: EMOTION COMMOTION

Concept/ Description: Expressing emotions is a normal part of human behavior.

Objective: To be the first group to successfully identify the emotions enacted.

Materials: Emotion Commotion Cards (one set per group of five or six) (SM-24, 25) (laminate and cut for a permanent set)

Directions:
1. Divide the class into groups of five or six students.
2. Give each group a set of Emotion Commotion Cards and instruct them to place them face down.
3. On the teacher's signal, one member of the group will pick up a card and try to act out the emotion listed. The actor may not talk or write.
4. The group members call out their guesses and as soon as the exact word is called out, the next player chooses a card and acts it out.
5. Play proceeds until all sixteen cards have been guessed.
6. The first team to guess all sixteen emotions is declared the winner.
7. Discuss which emotions were most difficult to act out. Why?

Note: A set of blank cards is provided if you wish to add more emotions.

EMOTION COMMOTION CARDS (SM-24)

HAPPY	**DISGUSTED**
FURIOUS	**NERVOUS**
AFRAID	**IN GREAT PAIN**
IMPATIENT	**DEPRESSED**

EMOTION COMMOTION CARDS (SM-25)

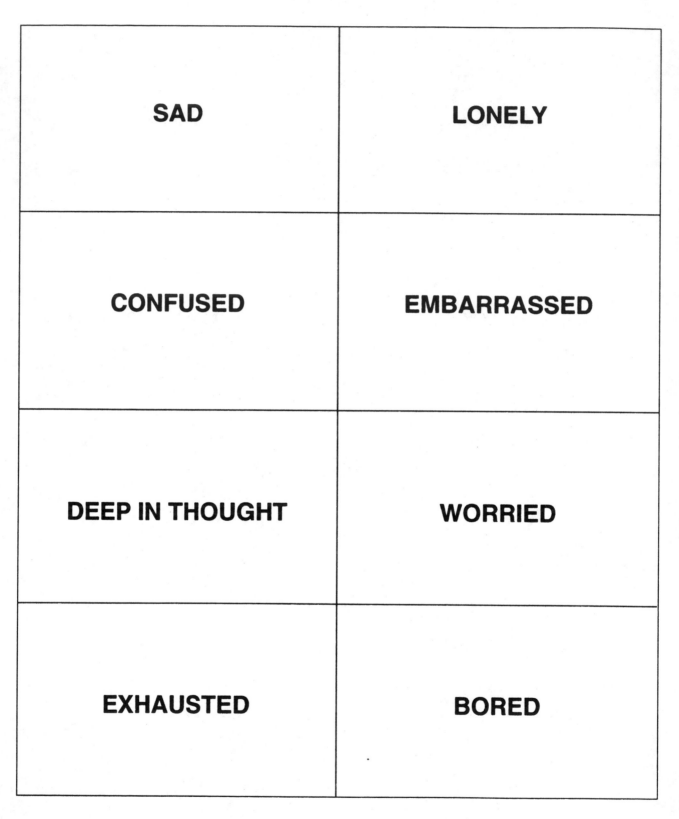

SAD	**LONELY**
CONFUSED	**EMBARRASSED**
DEEP IN THOUGHT	**WORRIED**
EXHAUSTED	**BORED**

EMOTION COMMOTION CARDS (SM-26)

EMOTIONAL ROLLER COASTER (SM-27)

DIRECTIONS: Our emotions may change drastically throughout the course of a day. For one day, plot your emotions by placing an *X* in the box that best describes your emotions at each given time. At the end of the day, connect the *X*s with a red line. How much did your emotions change?

TIME OF DAY

	8	9	10	11	12	1	2	3	4	5	6
HAPPY											
SAD											
ANGRY											
ANNOYED											
AFRAID											

Name _____ **Date** _____

EMOTIONAL OUTLETS (SM-28)

DIRECTIONS: In each box, write what you do when you experience the emotion listed. Include both constructive and nonconstructive behavior.

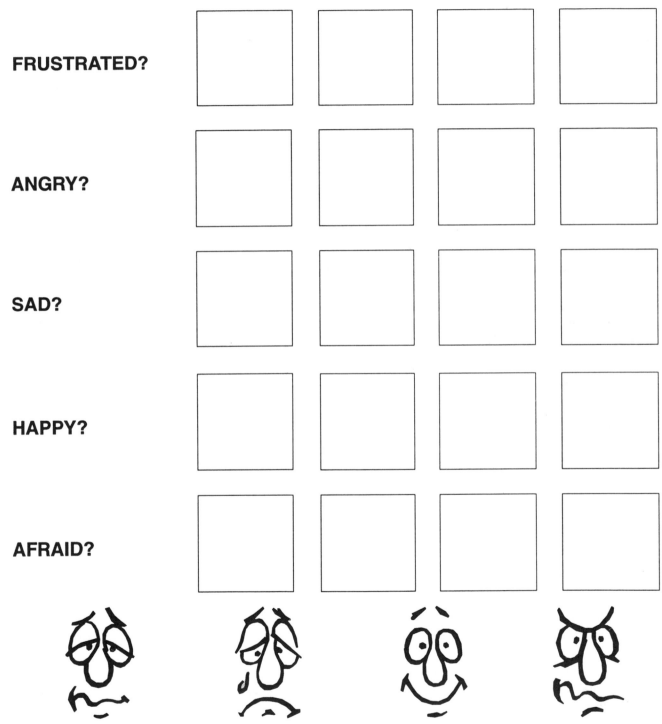

FRUSTRATED?

ANGRY?

SAD?

HAPPY?

AFRAID?

STRESS & ILLNESS* (SM-29)

DIRECTIONS: Check each event that you've experienced over the past year. Each event represents a change in a person's life. Whether it is a positive or negative change, it may threaten one's sense of security. Next to each event is a number representing the "stress points" that the event is worth. After you have checked the list, add the stress point values and refer to the SCORING FOR STRESS & ILLNESS worksheet to interpret your score.

_____	1. Being pregnant and unwed	92
_____	2. Death of a parent	87
_____	3. Death of a sister or brother	85
_____	4. Death of a friend	83
_____	5. Divorce or separation of parents	77
_____	6. Becoming an unwed father	77
_____	7. Becoming involved with alcohol or other drugs	76
_____	8. Family member's alcohol or other drug problem	75
_____	9. Having a parent go to jail for a year or more	75
_____	10. Having a change in acceptance by peers	67
_____	11. Discovering that you are adopted	64
_____	12. Loss or death of a pet	63
_____	13. Having a parent remarry	63
_____	14. Having a visible deformity	62
_____	15. Having a serious illness that requires hospitalization	58
_____	16. Going to a new school	56
_____	17. Moving to a new home	55
_____	18. Failing a grade in school	55
_____	19. Not making a team or extracurricular activity	54
_____	20. Having a parent become seriously ill	54
_____	21. Beginning to date	51
_____	22. Being suspended from school	50
_____	23. Having a newborn brother or sister	50
_____	24. Arguing more with parents	47
_____	25. Having an outstanding personal achievement	46
_____	26. Parents arguing more	46
_____	27. Having a parent lose his or her job	46
_____	28. A change in parents' financial status	45
_____	29. Being accepted to college	43
_____	30. Having a brother or sister leave home	37
_____	31. Death of a grandparent	36
_____	32. Having a grandparent move in	33
_____	33. Marriage of a brother or sister	30

_____

*Adapted from *HEALTH Choosing Wellness*, Second Edition, P. 49, © 1992 by Prentice Hall, Inc. Used by permission.

SCORING FOR STRESS & ILLNESS (SM-30)

What your score means:

150 and below: You have experienced little stress.
151-300: You have experienced moderate life change.
Over 300: Your life has changed greatly. According to experts you have a 50% greater chance of illness.

ANSWER THE FOLLOWING QUESTIONS:

1. Into which category does your score place you?

2. Are you satisfied or dissatisfied with your score?

3. In a paragraph, explain the kind of year you've had.

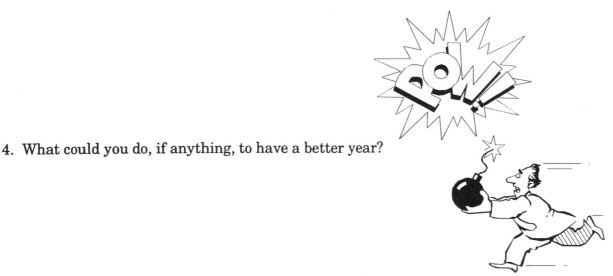

4. What could you do, if anything, to have a better year?

ACTIVITY 3: IT'S TRANSPARENT

Concept/ Description: People use various coping strategies to deal with unpleasant or painful circumstances.

Objective: To understand and give examples of some common defense mechanisms or coping strategies.

Materials: Overhead transparencies of Coping Strategies (SM-31 to SM-40)
Overhead projector
Screen or blank wall

Directions:
1. Prior to class, have sheets (SM-31 to SM-40) made into overhead transparencies using a thermal copy machine.
2. If that is unavailable, have the sheets laminated and display them at various points in the room.
3. Show each coping strategy and ask students to give examples from their own experiences or from the experiences of people they know.
4. Divide the class into groups of 4-5 and assign each group a coping strategy.
5. Give each group about 10 to 15 minutes to come up with a 1-minute skit showing an example of their assigned strategy.
6. Show the skits to the class.

DENIAL (SM-31)

Refusing to recognize an emotion or a problem

Assuming the qualities of someone you admire

COMPENSATION (SM-33)

**Making up for weakness in one area
by excelling in another area**

RATIONALIZATION (SM-34)

Making excuses for actions or feelings

PROJECTION (SM-35)

Putting your own faults onto someone else

DAYDREAMING (SM-36)

Fantasizing to escape unpleasant reality

DISPLACEMENT (SM-37)

Transferring emotions from the original source to another

REACTION FORMATION (SM-38)

Behaving in a manner opposite to the way you are feeling

REGRESSION (SM-39)

**Reverting to immature behavior
to express emotions**

Directing your energy into a useful rather than an unacceptable goal

COPING WITH EMOTIONS (SM-41)

Sometimes emotions become too much to handle. Often people use coping strategies (defense mechanisms) consciously or unconsciously. Sometimes coping strategies can protect you from painful events, but even if overused they can stunt emotional growth. If you depend on these strategies too much, you may not learn to express your true feelings.

DIRECTIONS: Below are common coping strategies and their definitions. After studying these, take the "I Hope I Can Cope" quiz (see SM-42).

1. DENIAL—refusing an emotion or problem.

   Ex. Your boyfriend/girlfriend breaks up with you, but you act as though nothing is wrong. When people ask if you are okay, you laugh and say you're not upset at all.

2. IDENTIFICATION—assuming the qualities of someone that you admire.

   Ex. You admire your older cousin so much that you begin to dress, talk, and act like him.

3. COMPENSATION—making up for weakness in one area by excelling in another area.

   Ex. You got cut from a sports team at school so you make up for it by becoming the captain of the debate team.

4. RATIONALIZATION—making excuses for actions or feelings.

   Ex. You copy the answers to a test from a classmate. You figure it's no big deal because it wasn't a major test.

5. PROJECTION—putting your own faults onto another person.

   Ex. You get benched during a hockey game because you are not playing well. You blame the coach, saying she didn't teach you the right things.

6. DAYDREAMING—fantasizing to escape unpleasant reality.

   Ex. You wish you were a good musician. You imagine being the lead singer in your own rock band.

7. DISPLACEMENT—transferring emotions from the original source to another.

   Ex. You are arguing with your parents so you slam your bedroom door.

8. REACTION FORMATION—behaving in a manner opposite to the way you are feeling.

   Ex. You feel guilty about drinking. To hide your feelings you brag to your friends about how much you drank.

9. REGRESSION—reverting to immature behavior to express emotions.

   Ex. You are mad at your sister for wearing your clothes. You scream and cry to your parents and run into your room.

10. SUBLIMATION—directing your energy into a useful rather than an unacceptable goal.

    Ex. You are a naturally aggressive person. You join the wrestling team.

"I HOPE I CAN COPE" QUIZ (SM-42)

DIRECTIONS: Read each situation and decide which coping strategy the person involved is using. (Refer to SM-41, *Coping With Emotions* if you need help.) Place the correct letter in the blank to the left.

_____ 1. Kati didn't get her way. She stomped up the steps, threw her stuffed animals around the room, and cried.

_____ 2. Rob got a terrible report card. He became the best basketball player on his team.

_____ 3. Kristin imagined herself scoring the winning goal in the state championship soccer game.

_____ 4. Jarred was fired from his summer job because he was always late. He said it was his mom's fault for not waking him up on time.

_____ 5. Mrs. Smith's husband died 3 months ago. She still sets his place at the dinner table.

_____ 6. Debbie feels guilty for stealing some jewelry. She shows the jewelry to her friends and brags about how she got it.

_____ 7. Danny got into a lot of arguments, so he decided to join the debate team.

_____ 8. Heather was furious with her sister, so she screamed at the family dog to get away from her.

_____ 9. Denise likes a certain rock group so she dresses and talks like they do.

_____ 10. Tony stole five packs of baseball cards at a card show. He figured it didn't matter because the vendor had thousands of packs.

a. Sublimation	f. Displacement
b. Regression	g. Denial
c. Reaction Formation	h. Rationalization
d. Compensation	i. Daydreaming
e. Projection	j. Identification

ACTIVITY 4: MENTAL HEALTH PROBLEMS

Concepts/
Description: There are many causes for mental disorders. There are many different types of mental disorders.

Objective: To research and discuss some of the many mental disorders, their signs, and symptoms.

Materials: Paper
Pencils or pens

Directions:
1. Schedule a period in the library.
2. Divide the class into research groups of three or four.
3. Assign each group one of the topics below and ask them to research it.
4. Ask students to report their findings back to the class.
5. Discuss treatments and possible coping strategies.

LIST OF TOPICS TO ASSIGN

Depression
Suicide
Schizophrenia
Seasonal Affective Disorder (SAD)
Neurosis
Psychosis
Phobias
Anorexia
Bulimia

Name _____   Date _____

DEPRESSION (SM-43)

DIRECTIONS: Listed below are some common symptoms associated with depression. In groups of four or five, come up with a list of things a depressed person could do to help lift him- or herself out of his or her depression before it slips into a dangerous stage. Group your suggestions into four categories: social contacts, communication, places to get help, becoming involved.

Signs and Symptoms:

excessive sleep or insomnia
loss of control
withdrawal
eating problems
loss of memory or concentration
disinterest in work or school
physical pains
self-doubts and self-criticism

irritability
feelings of loneliness
excessive use of alcohol or other drugs
thought of suicide
attempts at suicide
feelings of hopelessness
feelings of guilt and sadness
loss of interest in friends

SOCIAL CONTACTS

COMMUNICATION

PLACES TO GET HELP

BECOMING INVOLVED

Name _____   Date _____

MENTAL DISORDERS SEEK 'N FIND (SM-44)

DIRECTIONS: Listed below are some clues that will help you find the key vocabulary words that are associated with mental disorders. Once you've figured out the disorder, circle it in the seek 'n find puzzle. Words may be vertical, horizontal, diagonal, forwards or backwards.

A	P	A	R	A	N	O	I	A	A	L	I	G	A	S	C	A	L	M	T	O	T	E	C	A	A	L	A
E	S	B	D	S	A	E	P	L	D	A	D	H	M	I	D	R	L	A	O	B	E	V	Z	I	T	O	B
T	Y	C	N	L	E	I	M	E	O	M	I	N	A	N	W	O	A	P	Z	O	L	I	S	Z	Y	U	K
R	C	A	I	E	P	B	O	T	A	S	W	X	O	D	N	S	U	G	H	A	R	N	I	X	H	T	W
G	H	I	N	D	C	L	C	F	G	H	A	I	R	D	N	O	H	C	O	P	Y	H	W	A	T	S	I
H	O	T	G	A	E	E	T	H	E	I	J	K	L	P	M	U	V	E	L	L	I	T	H	Y	A	K	H
I	S	L	M	I	D	E	O	E	F	A	B	R	G	E	A	I	N	E	R	H	P	O	Z	I	H	C	S
E	I	D	E	T	T	H	E	S	F	O	C	I	C	O	O	N	R	S	I	I	L	R	R	E	R	E	D
W	S	L	A	R	C	I	D	S	E	O	U	R	S	E	T	F	E	C	L	A	Y	S	M	U	S	A	R
B	F	E	X	E	R	E	I	Y	O	U	H	L	I	V	O	T	I	N	B	D	R	S	T	A	I	K	C
O	E	T	R	E	A	V	C	D	A	T	Y	L	E	T	E	R	B	D	O	U	U	G	A	L	E	N	I
G	D	B	H	E	L	O	I	A	N	E	R	I	C	S	O	F	G	M	N	I	N	R	Y	K	I	N	D
N	W	C	T	T	D	S	U	L	L	A	O	B	S	A	T	O	L	A	O	P	S	T	H	E	E	A	W
I	L	S	R	A	U	E	S	E	I	I	R	I	I	O	A	N	E	R	N	Q	E	S	H	E	B	J	Z
T	H	K	Y	L	F	C	O	L	Y	T	S	C	A	N	N	R	E	L	O	I	V	S	E	D	N	A	O
A	I	I	D	I	N	G	Y	E	T	O	A	C	E	E	G	B	O	L	I	F	C	E	Y	R	K	C	R
L	T	S	P	U	E	O	N	N	R	P	A	H	M	L	U	E	D	D	H	C	K	S	U	G	P	A	E
M	S	I	Z	Z	R	S	I	U	N	O	S	O	P	N	A	N	N	Y	G	D	I	R	G	U	E	E	X
O	I	S	E	L	A	G	E	N	I	R	F	N	I	T	N	E	O	T	S	N	A	I	L	I	R	L	D
P	M	O	S	S	T	N	A	I	I	H	C	Z	S	E	E	N	R	G	H	A	F	C	A	N	A	S	O

Clues:

o _ _ _ _ _ c **disorder** (disorder caused by a physical illness or injury that affects the brain)

_ **yp** _ _ _ _ _ _ **r** _ _ (fear of presumed illness)

_ **u** _ **cid** _ (taking one's own life)

n _ _ _ **os** _ **s** (anxiety or fear keeps a person from functioning normally)

psy _ _ _ _ _ **s** (perception of reality is so distorted that a person cannot function at all)

_ **e** _ **r** _ **ss** _ _ _ (feelings of loneliness, hopelessness, and withdrawal from others)

p _ _ _ **n** _ **ia** (an overwhelming fear that interferes with one's ability to function normally)

_ **chi** _ _ _ _ _ _ _ **ia** (split personality)

51

UNDERSTANDING YOURSELF

- **Identifying Traits**

- **Appearance and Self-Confidence**

- **Values**

- **Success and Confidence**

- **Self Discovery**

- **Personality**

STRENGTHS & WEAKNESSES (SM-45)

DIRECTIONS: Complete the sentences below:

1. I feel good when _____ says I _____

_____.

2. I feel left out when _____.

3. I get angry when_____ corrects me

   on _____.

4. It's disappointing when _____ doesn't notice.

5. No matter how hard I try, I never_____

_____.

6. LIST YOUR STRENGTHS AND WEAKNESSES BELOW:

STRENGTHS	**WEAKNESSES**
_____	_____
_____	_____
_____	_____
_____	_____
_____	_____
_____	_____
_____	_____

WHO ARE YOU? (SM-46)

DIRECTIONS: Mark each statement with a *T* for TRUE or an *F* for FALSE to describe traits about yourself. Discuss with your classmates.

_____ 1. I am usually very friendly to others.

_____ 2. I can usually accept other people for what they are without trying to change them.

_____ 3. I often hurt other people's feelings.

_____ 4. I am very competitive and aggressive.

_____ 5. I am a quiet, reserved, laid-back person.

_____ 6. I like to be the leader and run things.

_____ 7. I am very energetic.

_____ 8. I prefer to be with other people than alone.

_____ 9. I get a great deal of exercise.

_____10. I practically never lose my temper.

_____11. I often get my feelings hurt by other people.

_____12. I love physical adventure and some risk or chance.

_____13. I need at least 8 hours of sleep a night.

_____14. I usually let others take the lead.

_____15. I have a loud, strong voice.

_____16. My friends consider me a good listener.

_____17. I find it difficult to relax at times.

_____18. I have a good relationship and open communication with my parents.

_____19. I usually tell people what I think.

_____20. I will avoid a confrontation if at all possible.

_____21. I dislike noise and loud voices.

_____22. I prefer to be alone when I am upset.

_____23. I get my work done on time.

_____24. I am self-conscious about my appearance.

_____25. I am very intense about my grades and schoolwork.

_____26. I worry a lot.

_____27. I am very sensitive to pain.

_____28. I am frequently tired or fatigued.

_____29. I like outdoor sports and camping.

_____30. Material things are very important to me.

WHAT'S MY LINE? (SM-47)

DIRECTIONS: Place an *X* on each line indicating where you rate yourself. In which areas are you satisfied or dissatisfied? What could you do to improve the areas that need improvement?

Total Slob
Room should be condemned.

Neat Freak
Room is spotless...you could eat off the floor.

└─────────────────────────────────────┘

Hot Head
Get angry about every little thing.

Cool Operator
Takes a great deal to get me angry.

└─────────────────────────────────────┘

Class Clown
I say things that usually
make others laugh.

Quiet and Reserved
I rarely tell jokes.

└─────────────────────────────────────┘

Total Jock
I love playing sports.

Non-Athletic
I am not the least bit
interested in sports.

└─────────────────────────────────────┘

Optimist
I see the glass half-full.

Pessimist
I see the glass half-empty.

└─────────────────────────────────────┘

Leader

Follower

└─────────────────────────────────────┘

Health Fanatic
Exercise and healthy foods
are a must.

Couch Potato
TV and some junk food for me.

└─────────────────────────────────────┘

Chatterbox
I love to talk.

All Ears
I'd rather listen.

└─────────────────────────────────────┘

Gossiper
I love to tell
"juicy" stories.

My Lips Are Sealed
I would never spread rumors.

└─────────────────────────────────────┘

Forgiving
I am able to forgive
and forget.

Grudge-Holder
I hold grudges for years.

└─────────────────────────────────────┘

Name _____ **Date** _____

QUALITY TIME (SM-48)

DIRECTIONS: List all the qualities that you like in other people in the first column. Then, list all the qualities that you dislike in other people in the second column. When you are finished place a + next to each quality that YOU have (look at both columns). Next, circle any quality that you wish you possessed. Finally, with a partner, discuss how a person could turn a negative quality into a positive one.

QUALITIES THAT I LIKE IN OTHERS	QUALITIES THAT I DISLIKE IN OTHERS
_____	_____
_____	_____
_____	_____
_____	_____
_____	_____
_____	_____
_____	_____
_____	_____
_____	_____
_____	_____
_____	_____
_____	_____
_____	_____
_____	_____

HOW DO I LOOK? (SM-49)

DIRECTIONS: Fill in the chart below. First list physical qualities that people might make fun of, then write a + if that attribute can be changed or a − if it cannot. Research and list the approximate cost of changing that physical attribute, then explain the possible consequences of doing so.

PHYSICAL QUALITY	ABILITY TO CHANGE	APPROX. COST	CONSEQUENCES
Large nose	+	$2,000-$6,000	Difficulty breathing

Name _____ **Date** _____

MIRROR, MIRROR ON THE WALL (SM-50)

DIRECTIONS: How you feel about your body can affect your self-confidence and attitude toward life. Rank each body part according to the way you perceive yourself, then add up your score below.

	Very Satisfied (4)	Satisfied (3)	Dissatisfied (2)	Very Unhappy (1)
Height				
Weight				
Thighs				
Calves				
Hips				
Arms				
Shoulders				
Skin				
Hair				
Eyes				
Ears				
Nose				
Mouth				
Stomach				

How do you rate yourself?
44–56 You are very satisfied.
34–43 You are satisfied.
24–33 You are somewhat dissatisfied.
14–23 Think positive, you probably look better than you think!

Name _____ **Date**_____

VALUES RANKING (SM-51)

DIRECTIONS: Rank the qualities or values listed below in order of importance to you. Number 1 would be MOST IMPORTANT and number 28 would be LEAST IMPORTANT. Write the quality on the line next to its corresponding number. Be sure to rank order ALL the values listed.

VALUES

...a nice car?

be a good friend to others
be famous
be a leader
have a sense of humor
serve my community
serve my country
make a lot of money
be intelligent
get married
be healthy
be in good shape
be attractive
have a pet
have a close relationship

have nice clothes
have a nice car
get a good job
be independent
be close to my family
have a lot of friends
have strong faith in God
do what is morally right
have children
work with children
be a good athlete
have enough money to feel secure
communicate well
be in love

©1993 by The Center for Applied Research in Education

1 _____
2 _____
3 _____
4 _____
5 _____
6 _____
7 _____
8 _____
9 _____
10 _____
11 _____
12 _____
13 _____
14 _____

15 _____
16 _____
17 _____
18 _____
19 _____
20 _____
21 _____
22 _____
23 _____
24 _____
25 _____
26 _____
27 _____
28 _____

Name _____   Date _____

WHERE DO I STAND? (SM-52)

DIRECTIONS: Using a red pencil or a marker, color in the thermometers to indicate how strongly you feel about each statement. Coloring in the entire thermometer would indicate that you are in total disagreement with the statement, while leaving it blank would indicate that you are in total agreement. Anything in between would indicate how strongly you agree or disagree.

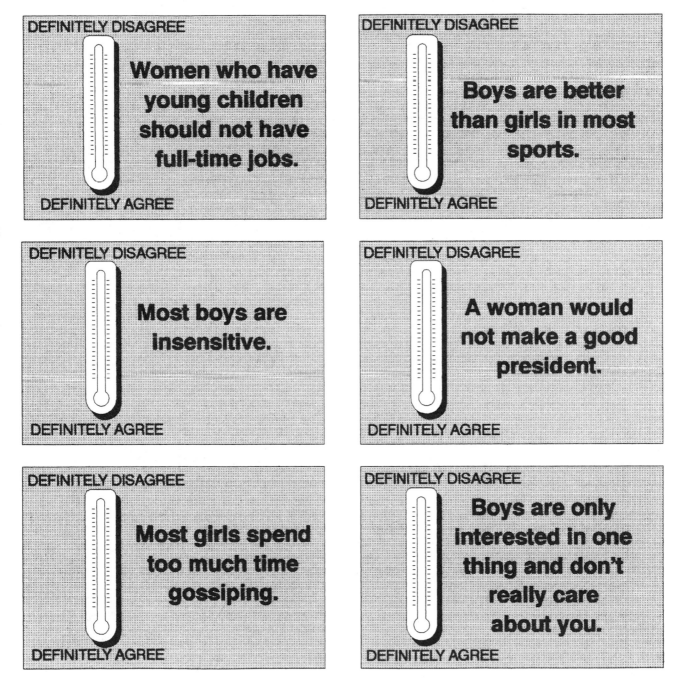

DEFINITELY DISAGREE	DEFINITELY DISAGREE
Women who have young children should not have full-time jobs.	**Boys are better than girls in most sports.**
DEFINITELY AGREE	DEFINITELY AGREE
DEFINITELY DISAGREE	DEFINITELY DISAGREE
Most boys are insensitive.	**A woman would not make a good president.**
DEFINITELY AGREE	DEFINITELY AGREE
DEFINITELY DISAGREE	DEFINITELY DISAGREE
Most girls spend too much time gossiping.	**Boys are only interested in one thing and don't really care about you.**
DEFINITELY AGREE	DEFINITELY AGREE

Name _____ **Date** _____

BRANCHING OUT (SM-53)

DIRECTIONS: Though it may be difficult at first, list at least fifteen "successes" that you have had throughout your life. Be specific. Write the age you were, what you did, and how you felt. Think of times when you felt proud, happy, or satisfied knowing that you did well. After you have written your successes, fill out the SUCCESS GRID (SM-54).

EXAMPLE: When I was thirteen, my baseball team had a winning season. I hit twelve homeruns that year. I felt proud that I contributed to the team's success.

SUCCESSES

1.

2.

3.

4.

5.

6.

7.

8.

9.

10.

11.

12.

13.

14.

15.

Name _____ **Date** _____

SUCCESS GRID (SM-54)

DIRECTIONS: Refer to the branching out activity (SM-53), in which you listed fifteen of your successes. Read each success story again and place a check next to the quality that the particular story highlights. What three qualities received the most checks? Write those qualities on the roots of the success tree (SM-55). Write the rest of the qualities in the apples.

Artistic Ability	
Athletic Ability	
Perserverence	
Creativity	
Caring for Others	
Good Communications	
Solving Problems	
Writing	
Intelligence	
Courage	
Strength of Character	

Write your top three qualities below:

1. _____

2. _____

3. _____

SUCCESS TREE (SM-55)

BELIEVE IT OR NOT! (SM-56)

Our thoughts and beliefs can make a harmless situation very stressful. Our beliefs are influenced by our family, friends, environment, education, and religion. Sometimes negative or SELF-DEFEATING THOUGHTS are difficult to change, but with practice they can be changed.

DIRECTIONS: Listed below are some common examples of NEGATIVE SELF-TALK. Next to each negative thought, write an appropriate form of POSITIVE SELF-TALK. Two examples are provided.

NEGATIVE SELF-TALK

1. To be a worthwhile person, I should be good at everything.

2. I should be liked, or approved of, by almost everyone.

3. Every problem must have the perfect solution, and if it doesn't, it's really bad.

4. People never change.

5. Everything I do must lead to an immediate reward or payoff.

6. I can't help how I feel...and I'm feeling miserable.

7. If there is any possibility that something could go wrong, I should worry about it a lot.

8. It is easier to avoid than to face problems and responsibilities.

POSITIVE SELF-TALK

1. I can't expect to be perfect at everything.

2. No one is liked by everyone. It is unrealistic to think that everyone will like me.

Name _____ **Date** _____

A VOTE OF CONFIDENCE (SM-57)

DIRECTIONS: Take the self-confidence test below by circling the number that indicates where you rank yourself for each item. Add up the scores and see where you stand according to the key. Are you as confident as you'd like to be?

	NEVER	SOMETIMES	USUALLY
1. In general, I am happy with myself.	1 2	3 4	5
2. I am pleased with my personal appearance.	1 2	3 4	5
3. I am pleased with my relationships with others.	1 2	3 4	5
4. I am able to accept criticism without getting upset.	1 2	3 4	5
5. If things don't go my way, I keep trying.	1 2	3 4	5
6. I am happy when other people find success.	1 2	3 4	5
7. I am willing to ask for help if I need it.	1 2	3 4	5
8. I like the challenge of trying new things.	1 2	3 4	5
9. I feel comfortable meeting new people.	1 2	3 4	5
10. I have goals and expectations for myself.	1 2	3 4	5

KEY:

41–50 You have great confidence in yourself.
31–40 You are somewhat satisfied with yourself and your abilities.
21–30 You lack some self-confidence.
10–20 It can't be THAT bad. Cheer up and find some good in yourself!

ACTIVITY 5: A PAT ON THE BACK

**Concept/
Description:**
Receiving and giving compliments can build self-esteem.

Objective:
To have students recognize and acknowledge each other's strengths.

Materials:
Large sheets of light colored construction paper
Masking tape
Crayons

Directions:
1. Have each person tape a piece of construction paper to his or her back.
2. Give each student a crayon.
3. Students stand and walk around the room. Each person is to write at least one positive comment on every other person's sheet. Comments should highlight that person's strengths.
4. When all are finished, ask each student to remove the paper and look at it.
5. Ask if anyone had something written that surprised them. Discuss.

funny

caring

creative

intelligent

easy to talk to!

FISHING FOR COMPLIMENTS (SM-58)

DIRECTIONS: We all need compliments once in a while. Get in groups of five or six and pass this paper to each person in your group. When you receive a paper, in the spaces provided, write a compliment to the person whose name is at the top. Give the paper back to its owner. How does it feel to receive so many compliments?

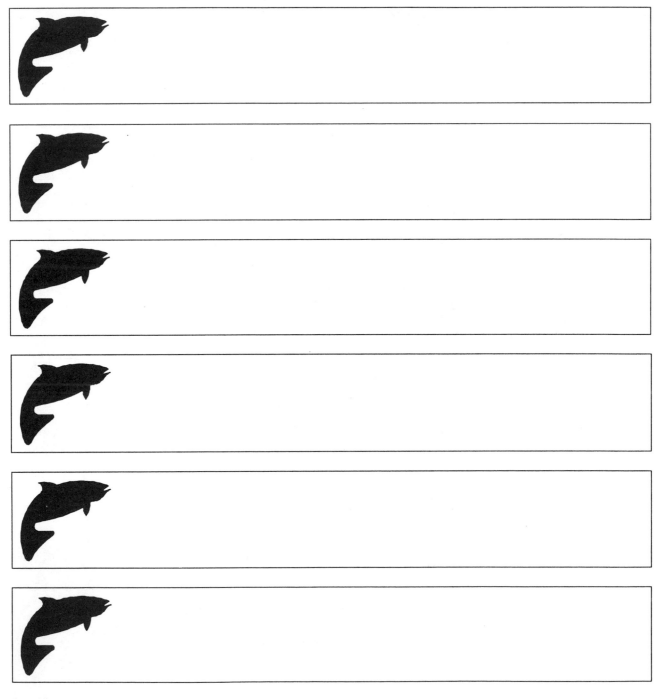

"PRESENTS" OF MIND (SM-59)

DIRECTIONS: On the gift tags below, write the names of six people to whom you would give a present. In the boxes, write the gift you would give that person, keeping in mind that money is no object. The gift can be material, such as a new home or car, or it can be intangible, such as love, understanding, or patience.

LIFT YOUR BURDENS (SM-60)

DIRECTIONS: What burdens would you lift from family and friends if you could? On the forklift are five boxes. On each box, write the name of the person you would like to help, and the burden you would like to lift from them. For example, you could list your grandmother and say you would like to remove her pain from a heart ailment, or list a neighbor and say you would like to take away his anger from a recent job loss.

HEAVY LOAD

©1993 by The Center for Applied Research in Education

Name _____ **Date** _____

WHAT'S IN A NAME? (SM-61)

DIRECTIONS: Write your first and last name vertically in the space provided. Use the letters to write words that describe your positive qualities. Compare yours to your classmates. An example is given below:

P	**atient**
A	**ccepting**
T	**rustworthy**
S	**ociable**
M	**ellow**
I	**ntelligent**
T	**reats people with respect**
H	**umorous**

Try your name below:

I'm glad I have a short name...

INNER CIRCLE (SM-62)

DIRECTIONS: In the circles below, list the people to whom you feel closest. The person next
to you would be the closest, and so on. Then, using colored pencils or markers,
color each circle with a color that reminds you of that person. In the space under
the circles, write a paragraph about the person to whom you feel closest.
Underline the words you use to describe that person. Finally, put a circle around
any word that could also be used to describe you.

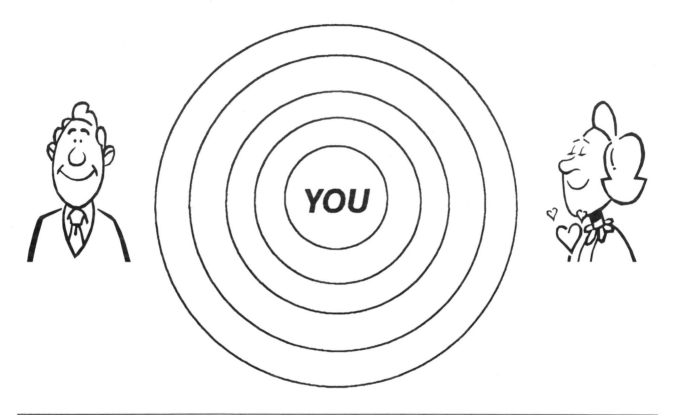

_____
_____
_____
_____
_____
_____
_____
_____
_____
_____

PICTURE THIS (SM-63)

DIRECTIONS: Imagine what your life will be like in the future. In each box, fill in the information requested for the age given.

AGE	WHERE I LIVE	WHAT I DO	PEOPLE CLOSE TO ME
NOW			
25			
35			
50			
65			

WIFE, KIDS...

ACTIVITY 6: WHAT DO YOU SAY?

Concept/
Description: Students play a game that will help to foster self-discovery and communication.

Objective: To answer the questions honestly and have others do the same.

Materials: What Do You Say? cards (SM-64, 65)
(laminate and cut into decks; have one deck per group)

Directions:
1. Divide the class into groups of five or six and have them sit in circles.
2. Give a deck of What Do You Say? cards to each group.
3. Each person picks a card and reads it silently.
4. Starting with a volunteer (or you may assign one person to start), read the question aloud and answer it.
5. The person who answered may then choose one other person to answer the same question.
6. Continue the procedure until all have read their cards, then choose new cards and repeat the process.

   Note: At any time, a person may choose to pass on his or her topic and choose a new card. Some additional blank cards are provided so group members can add their own cards, if they wish.

WHAT DO YOU SAY? CARDS (SM-64)

Suppose someone gave you $500 right now. What would you do with it? **1**	Suppose your best friend had bad breath. Would you tell him or her? If so, what would you say? If not, why not? **2**	If you could take a potion that would allow you to live for 150 more years without illness, would you take it? Why or why not? **3**
If you could know the exact date of your death, would you want to know? Why or why not? **4**	What bothers you most about the opposite sex? **5**	If your son or daughter told you that he or she might have a sexually transmitted disease, what would you say or do? **6**
If you found a $100 bill on the ground outside a bank, what would you do? **7**	If you could be any animal for a day, what would you be? Why? **8**	Would you kill a puppy if by doing so it could save a homeless person's life? **9**
Finish this sentence: "The first impression most people have of me is ____." **10**	If you could trade places with anyone in the world for one day, who would you be? Why? **11**	What is the scariest thing that ever happened to you? **12**

WHAT DO YOU SAY? CARDS (SM-65)

Tell something that you did that made you feel especially proud. **13**	Talk about the best teacher you have ever had. **14**	If you could go on an all-expenses-paid trip to anywhere in the world, where would you go? **15**
What do you think is the biggest problem facing the world today? **16**	What is the meanest thing you ever saw someone do? Did you do anything about it? **17**	If you could bring a famous person to dinner, whom would you bring? Why? **18**
If someone you had just met had a piece of food caught in his or her teeth, would you bring it to his or her attention? If so, what would you do or say? **19**	If you could change any one thing about yourself, what would you change? **20**	What is your favorite song? Why do you like it? **21**
Name three things that you dislike about this school. **22**	Finish this sentence: "I feel bad when_____." **23**	Describe the "perfect date." **24**

WHAT DO YOU SAY? BLANK CARDS (SM-66)

ACTIVITY 7: IT'S IN THE BAG!

**Concept/
Description:** Students learn about each other by bringing in objects that mean something to them, while others try to guess to whom they belong.

Objective: To match each object to its owner, then discuss the meaning of each.

Materials: One large paper grocery store bag per group of six
Paper and pens or pencils
Marker

Directions:
1. Direct students to bring to class an object that will help to describe something about themselves. The object must fit completely in the grocery bag.
2. Divide the class into groups by counting off by six.
3. Number the grocery bags from 1 to 6 and write the number on each bag with a marker.
4. Place the open bags around the room and have students walk around the room and place their objects in the bag corresponding to their group number. Tell them not to allow anyone to see their objects as they place them in the bag.
5. When everyone is through, ask the class to meet in their groups. Give each group its own bag.
6. Direct the groups to empty the bags in front of them.
7. Have each group member try to match the objects to their owners by writing their guesses on a piece of paper.
8. Finally, have groups discuss their guesses with each other to determine to whom each object belongs and why. Ask each person to take a minute to explain why his or her object was brought in.

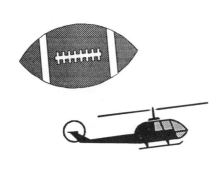

Name _____   **Date** _____

FRONT PAGE (SM-67)

DIRECTIONS: Drawn below is a sample layout of the front page of a newspaper. Design a newspaper highlighting YOURSELF. Include your greatest accomplishment, a self-portrait of you doing something that you enjoy, headlines, etc. In the box at the top, give your newspaper a name.

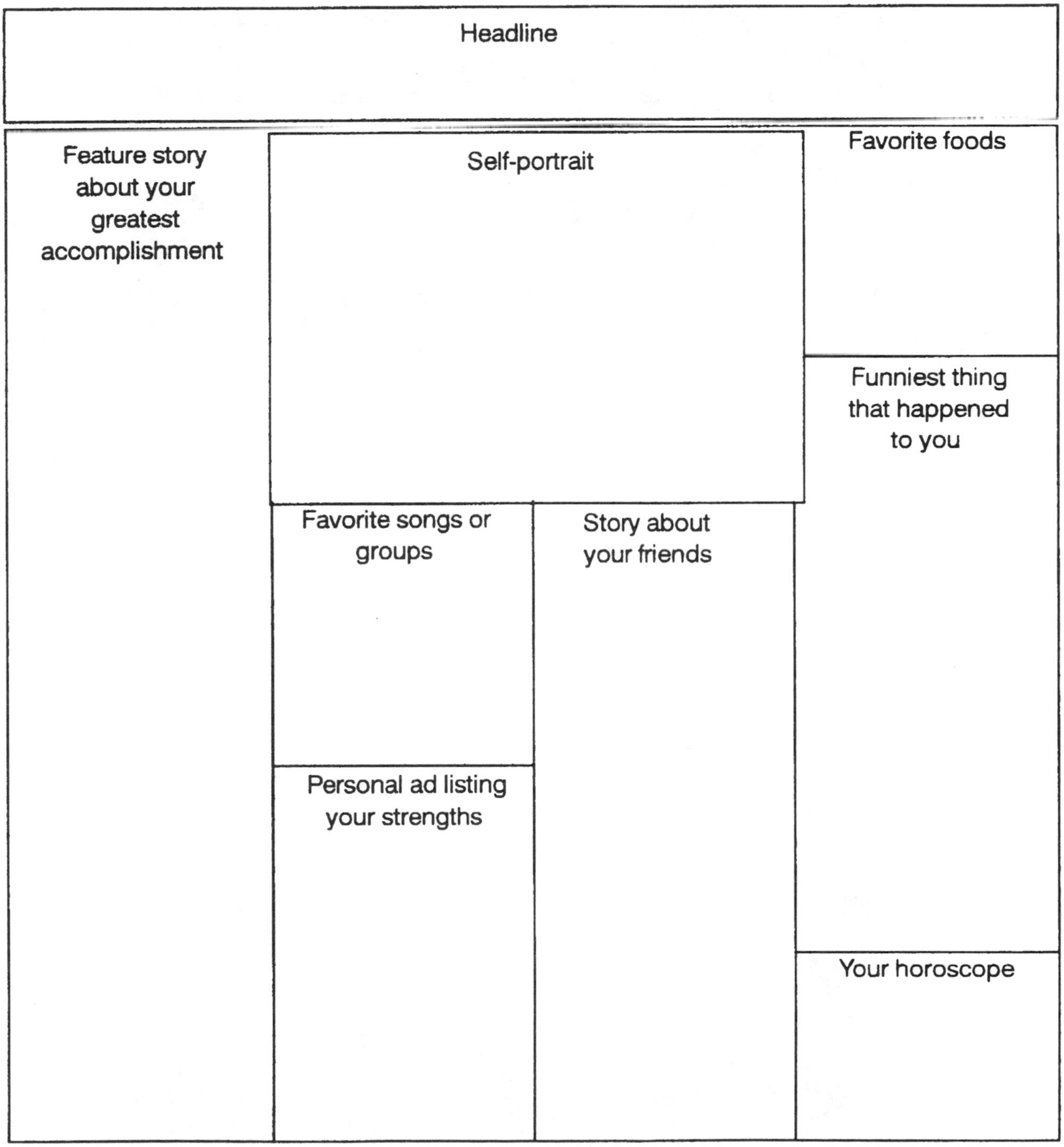

Headline

Feature story about your greatest accomplishment	Self-portrait	Favorite foods
		Funniest thing that happened to you
	Favorite songs or groups	Story about your friends	
	Personal ad listing your strengths		
			Your horoscope

NOW HEAR THIS! (SM-68)

DIRECTIONS: In the space below, draw or write a news flash highlighting something that you someday hope to accomplish, for example: "Dan Brown Completes the Boston Marathon in Record Time." Then write a spot announcement describing the accomplishment.

IT'S ALL IN YOUR HEAD (SM-69)

DIRECTIONS: What do you spend your time thinking about? The picture of the head is divided into sections. In each section, write or draw what you spend the most time thinking about. Compare your paper to a classmate's.

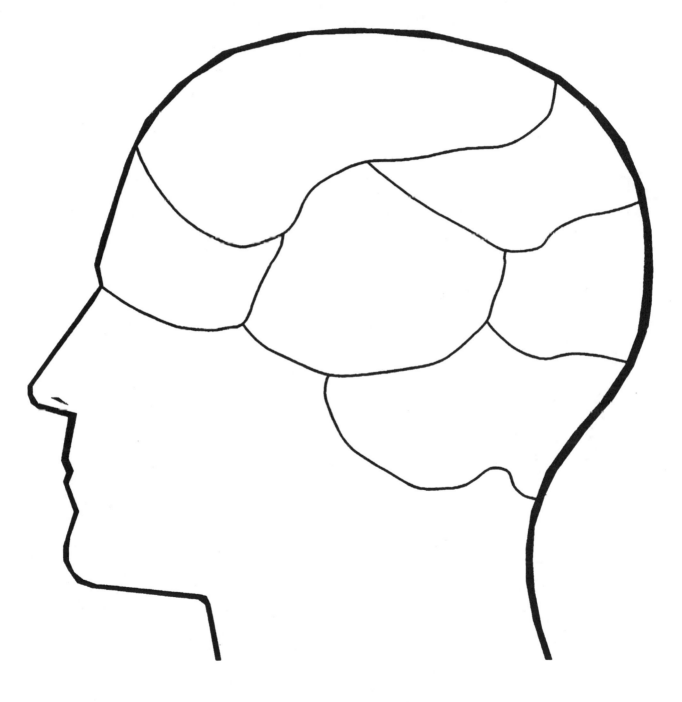

ACTIVITY 8: AGREE WITH ME

Concept/ Description: Students play a game and attempt to match answers with other group members.

Objective: To be the first person in the group to reach the finish.

Materials: Agree With Me gameboard (one for every student)(SM-70)
Forty-two Agree With Me cards per group (laminate and cut) (SM-71, 72)
Envelope to hold the cards
One die per group
Pens or pencils
Scrap paper (each player may use notebook paper)

Directions:

1. Give each player an Agree With Me gameboard.

2. Divide the class into groups of four or five and have each group sit together.

3. Give each group an envelope containing forty-two Agree With Me cards and one die.

"We can each each move two spaces..."

4. One player rolls the die and moves the corresponding number of spaces. (Players can mark their own sheets by making a light *X* in the space.)

5. Each player follows the directions on the gameboard.

6. If a player lands on a question mark, that player draws one of the Agree With Me cards that have been placed face down in a pile.

7. The player drawing the card reads the card aloud. All players then have one minute to write down as many answers as they can.

8. When the minute is up (a group member can time the group), the person who landed on the question mark reads his or her answers one by one. Any time someone else agrees with the answer read, they say so, and anyone with matching answers places a checkmark next to the answer. Each player, in turn, then reads any answers that have not been said yet. Once again, any time a player matches another player, each player receives a check.

9. Each player then counts the number of checkmarks for that question and moves the number of spaces on the board. Play proceeds clockwise.

10. The first person to reach the finish line is declared the winner.

Note: Only the person who rolled the die picks a card. Any other time you land on a question mark, you ignore it.

AGREE WITH ME GAMEBOARD (SM-70)

AGREE WITH ME GAME CARDS (SM-71)

FAVORITE FOODS	MOST DISGUSTING FOODS	BEST MUSICAL GROUPS
BEST TV SHOWS	WORST MUSICAL GROUPS	FUNNIEST PEOPLE
FAVORITE SUBJECTS	BEST SPORTS TO WATCH	WORST SPORTS TO WATCH ON TELEVISION
FAVORITE ACTORS	BEST PLACES TO GO ON VACATION	FUNNIEST PEOPLE IN THIS SCHOOL
BEST FAST FOOD PLACES	WORST FAST FOOD PLACES	FAVORITE ANIMALS
ANNOYING INSECTS	MOST ANNOYING SOUNDS	BORING PLACES TO GO OR BE
FAVORITE CARS	THINGS YOU HATE ABOUT MORNING	BEST SPORTS TO PLAY

AGREE WITH ME GAME CARDS (SM-72)

WORST SPORTS TO PLAY	WORST SMELLS	FAVORITE STORES
BEST THINGS ABOUT WINTER	WORST THING ABOUT PUBLIC RESTROOMS	WORST CRIMINALS
BEST MALE ATHLETES IN PRO SPORTS	BEST ATHLETES IN THIS SCHOOL	BEST THINGS ABOUT HALLOWEEN
WORST THINGS ABOUT SCHOOL	BEST THINGS ABOUT SCHOOL	BEST THINGS ABOUT HEALTH CLUBS
WORST GIFTS TO RECEIVE	BEST LOOKING PEOPLE YOU KNOW	BEST THINGS ABOUT CHRISTMAS
THINGS I DISLIKE ABOUT SIBLINGS	THINGS I ARGUE WITH MY PARENTS ABOUT	WORST JOBS
THINGS I HATE ABOUT DOCTOR'S VISITS	WORST HABITS PEOPLE HAVE	WORST CHORES

Name _____ **Date** _____

THE PERFECT DAY (SM-73)

DIRECTIONS: Describe in detail "The Perfect Day," if there could be one. What would you do? When would you do it? (Money is no object.) Read your day to a classmate.

MORNING

AFTERNOON

EVENING

Name _____ **Date** _____

WHEN I WAS YOUR AGE... (SM-74)

DIRECTIONS: Imagine that you area parent. You have a thirteen-year-old daughter and a twelve-year-old son. What important messages do you want to give your children as they enter adolescence? Write specific messages in the boxes below.

TO MY SON:

TO MY DAUGHTER:

REMEMBER ME? (SM-75)

DIRECTIONS: When your life is over, you will have met many people, been many places, and done many things. For what would you like to be remembered? Place your name on the line in the rectangle, then write your personal epitaph.

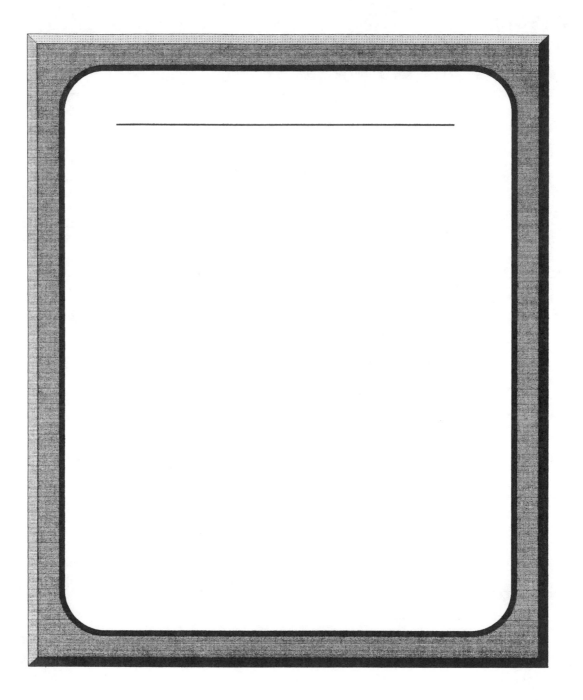

Name _____   Date _____

I LIKE THAT! (SM-76)

DIRECTIONS: In the spaces under "Activity" write down fifteen things you like to do, such as playing basketball, painting, going to the mall, etc. In each column, place an *X* if the heading applies. Then answer the questions at the bottom of the page.

Activity	Costs more than $5.00	Requires physical activity	Is done outdoors	Is done often	Is done with friends or family

Are most of the activities you enjoy expensive?

How many of the fifteen things you like to do require physical activity?

How many are done primarily outdoors?

Do you get to do the things you enjoy often? If not, why not?

Are most of the things you enjoy done with people or alone?

Name _____ **Date** _____

AN "I" FOR AN "I" (SM-77)

DIRECTIONS: Fill in the blanks for each statement listed below. Be sure to answer each one.

1. I believe_____.
2. I am _____.
3. I wish_____.
4. I believe_____.
5. I am _____.
6. I wish_____.
7. I believe_____.
8. I am _____.
9. I wish_____.
10. I believe_____.
11. I am _____.
12. I wish_____.
13. I believe_____.
14. I am _____.
15. I wish_____.

Write a paragraph about any one of your "I believe" answers:

I believe that all people should...

Name _____ **Date** _____

SAY WHAT? (SM-78)

DIRECTIONS: For each question below, put an *X* next to which best describes you. On the line below each question, write why.

ARE YOU?

1. _____ a Volkswagen or _____ a Jaguar?

_____

2. _____ a meadow or _____ a forest?

_____

3. _____ a hammer or _____ a nail?

_____

4. _____ a circle or _____ a triangle?

_____

5. _____ a bing or _____ a bong?

_____

6. _____ a table or _____ a chair?

_____

7. _____ a lion or _____ a rhino?

_____

8. _____ a comedy or _____ a tragedy?

_____

ASK A CLASSMATE WHAT HE OR SHE THINKS YOU ARE AND WHY.

Name _____   **Date** _____

PERSONAL COAT OF ARMS (SM-79)

DIRECTIONS: In each section of the Personal Coat of Arms, draw or cut out pictures that apply to each area of your life mentioned.

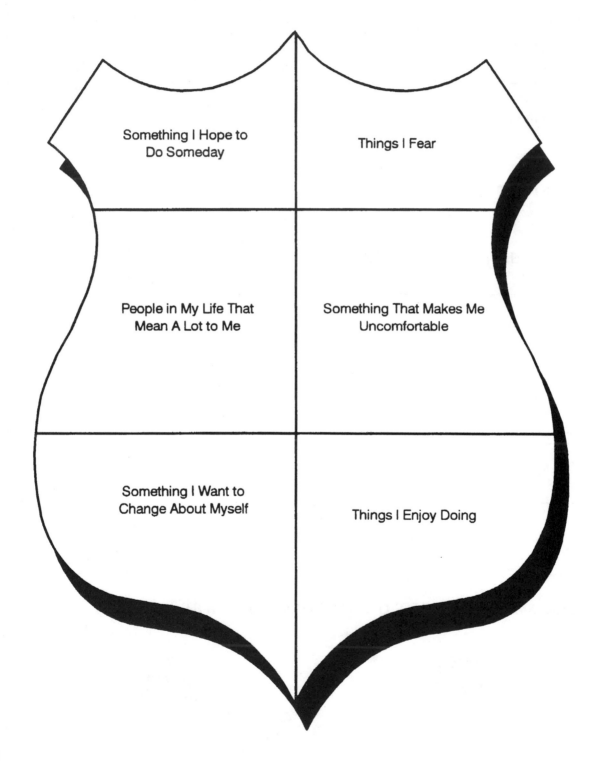

Something I Hope to Do Someday

Things I Fear

People in My Life That Mean A Lot to Me

Something That Makes Me Uncomfortable

Something I Want to Change About Myself

Things I Enjoy Doing

Name _____ **Date** _____

YOU'RE MY TYPE (SM-80)

DIRECTIONS: Read the explanations of the two personality types below, then take the test to determine which type you are.

Type A Personality

The Type A person is very competitive, often impatient, and feels that he or she must be successful. This person is aggressive and driven to work hard. They often feel that time is of the essence and, therefore, move and talk rapidly. Type A persons are usually impatient listeners. Because they are so driven, Type A persons are more at risk and susceptible to coronary heart disease and other stress-related diseases.

Type B Personality

The Type B person is more laid back and less hurried. This person is usually patient, noncompetitive, and nonaggressive.

WHICH TYPE ARE YOU?

DIRECTIONS: Place a + in the blank if the statement describes you and a − if it does not.

_____ 1. I become angry or aggravated if I have to stand in line for more than 10–15 minutes.

_____ 2. I try to do more than one thing at a time.

_____ 3. I try very hard to win while playing sports or games.

_____ 4. I feel guilty if I am doing nothing.

_____ 5. I hate to lose and become angry at myself or others if I do.

_____ 6. I speak, eat, and move quickly.

_____ 7. I interrupt people who talk slowly in order to speed things up.

_____ 8. I work better under pressure.

_____ 9. I have a strong need to be successful.

_____10. I set deadlines and schedules for myself.

> **SCORING.** If 6–10 statements describe you, you may be a Type A personality. If only a few describe you, you may be a Type B personality. Some people may be a combination depending on the circumstances. It is important that we are aware of ourselves and learn when and how to relax.

Name _____ **Date** _____

RORSCHACH TEST (SM-81)

DIRECTIONS: The Rorschach Ink Blot Test is a psychological test in which the subject is shown a series of ink blots of standard design. The responses of the subject give useful, if not always specific, information about the person's intelligence and emotional state. Though we cannot analyze each other's answers, look at each ink blot below and write what it looks like to you. Compare your answers to those of your classmates, then answer the questions at the bottom of this sheet.

Why are there so many different interpretations of the ink blots when we all saw the same design? What might influence a person's interpretation?

Name _____ **Date** _____

VOCABULARY CHALLENGE (SM-82)

DIRECTIONS: Match the words in the first column with their definition by placing the correct letter in the blank.

_____ 1. peer pressure
_____ 2. environment
_____ 3. psychologist
_____ 4. heredity
_____ 5. assertiveness
_____ 6. aggressive
_____ 7. self-concept
_____ 8. passivity
_____ 9. personality
_____ 10. compromise
_____ 11. cooperation
_____ 12. socialization
_____ 13. psychosis
_____ 14. neurosis
_____ 15. compulsive

a. the way you feel about yourself and how you think others feel about you
b. the passing of traits from parents to children
c. behaving in a forceful or threatening manner
d. traits that make one person different from another person
e. holding back your thoughts and feelings; giving in to another person
f. a trained professional who studies the human mind and behavior
g. the process by which children learn from people close to them about feelings, attitudes, and behavior
h. the need to conform to the expectations of friends
i. working together towards a common goal
j. a condition in which a person cannot function in the real world
k. your total surroundings
l. the ability to stand up for yourself and express your feelings in a nonthreatening way
m. giving up something in order to reach an agreement
n. a condition in which fear blocks a person's ability to function normally
o. an unreasonable need to behave in a certain way

VOCABULARY

ANSWER KEYS TO REPRODUCIBLES

ENVIRONMENTAL STRESSORS (SM-5)

DIRECTIONS: As a society we face many pressures that can affect our lives. These stressors include forms of pollution, conflict between nations, natural disasters, and economic changes. Fill in the crossword puzzle below to show some of these stressors.

©1993 by The Center for Applied Research in Education

ACROSS

1. Armed conflict between nations.
5. Excessive environmental noise from planes, autos, industry, etc. (two words)
6. A violent, whirling wind accompanied by a funnel-shaped cloud.
7. A large quantity of water overflowing onto what is normally dry land.
9. A rise in prices brought about by an increase in the ratio of currency and

DOWN

2. Unhealthy elements in the air we breathe. (two words)
3. Unhealthy and impure water supply. (two words)
4. A chemical change accompanied by the emission of heat, light, and flames.
8. A cyclone with winds exceeding 73 m.p.h. and usually covering a large area.

STRESSED OUT!! (SM-10)

DIRECTIONS: Unscramble the words and place them in the blanks to show the *PHYSICAL* signs and symptoms of stress. The letters in the circles will form a word that is a method of reducing stress. Write that hidden word in the blank at the bottom of the page.

1. **B R R Ⓔ A T H I N G**
2. **E Ⓧ C E S S**
3. **C H Ⓔ M I S T R Y**
4. **H E A Ⓡ T**
5. **M U S Ⓒ L E**
6. **D Ⓘ G E S T I O N**
7. **P R E Ⓢ S U R E**
8. **T E M P Ⓔ R A T U R E**

1. INCREASED RBTEAHNGI RATE

2. XESSCE SWEATING

3. CHANGES IN BLOOD HCMEITRYS

4. INCREASED RTEHA RATE

5. INCREASED LESCMU TENSION

6. DECREASED GDISTOINE

7. INCREASED BLOOD EEPSRSUR

8. DECREASED SKIN RTAEPETMRUE

HIDDEN WORD _____

"I HOPE I CAN COPE" QUIZ (SM-42)

DIRECTIONS: Read each situation and decide which coping strategy the person involved is using. (Refer to SM-41, *Coping With Emotions* if you need help. Place the correct letter in the blank to the left.

b 1. Kati didn't get her way. She stomped up the steps, threw her stuffed animals around the room, and cried.

d 2. Rob got a terrible report card. He became the best basketball player on his team.

i 3. Kristin imagined herself scoring the winning goal in the state championship soccer game.

e 4. Jarred was fired from his summer job because he was always late. He said it was his mom's fault for not waking him up on time.

g 5. Mrs. Smith's husband died 3 months ago. she still sets his place at the dinner table.

c 6. Debbie feels guilty for stealing some jewelry. She shows the jewelry to her friends and brags about how she got it.

a 7. Danny got into a lot of arguments, so he decided to join the debate team.

f 8. Heather was furious with her sister, so she screamed at the family dog to get away from her.

j 9. Denise likes a certain rock group so she dresses and talks like they do.

h 10. Tony stole five packs of baseball cards at a card show. He figured it didn't matter because the vendor had thousands of packs.

a. Sublimation	f. Displacement
b. Regression	g. Denial
c. Reaction Formation	h. Rationalization
d. Compensation	i. Daydreaming
e. Projection	j. Identification

MENTAL DISORDERS SEEK 'N FIND (SM-44)

DIRECTIONS: Listed below are some clues that will help you find the key vocabulary words that are associated with mental disorders. Once you've figured out the disorder, circle it in the seek 'n find puzzle. Words may be vertical, horizontal, diagonal, forwards or backwards.

Clues:

o _r_ _g_ _a_ _n_ _i_ c disorder (disorder caused by a physical illness or injury that affects the brain)

h y p o _c_ _h_ _o_ _n_ _d_ r _i_ _a_ (fear of presumed illness)

_s_ u _i_ cid _e_ (taking one's own life)

n _e_ _u_ _r_ os _i_ s (anxiety or fear keeps a person from functioning normally)

psy _c_ _h_ _o_ _s_ _i_ s (perception of reality is so distorted that a person cannot function at all)

_d_ e p r _e_ ss _i_ _o_ _n_ (feelings of loneliness, hopelessness, and withdrawal from others)

p _a_ _r_ _a_ no _o_ ia (an overwhelming fear that interferes with one's ability to function normally)

_s_ chi _z_ _o_ _p_ _h_ _r_ _e_ n ia (split personality)

101

VOCABULARY CHALLENGE (SM-82)

DIRECTIONS: Match the words in the first column with their definition by placing the correct letter in the blank.

<u>h</u> 1. peer pressure
<u>k</u> 2. environment
<u>f</u> 3. psychologist
<u>b</u> 4. heredity
<u>l</u> 5. assertiveness
<u>c</u> 6. aggressive
<u>a</u> 7. self-concept
<u>e</u> 8. passivity
<u>d</u> 9. personality
<u>m</u> 10. compromise
<u>i</u> 11. cooperation
<u>g</u> 12. socialization
<u>j</u> 13. psychosis
<u>n</u> 14. neurosis
<u>o</u> 15. compulsive

a. the way you feel about yourself and how you think others feel about you
b. the passing of traits from parents to children
c. behaving in a forceful or threatening manner
d. traits that make one person different from another person
e. holding back your thoughts and feelings; giving in to another person
f. a trained professional who studies the human mind and behavior
g. the process by which children learn from people close to them about feelings, attitudes, and behavior
h. the need to conform to the expectations of friends
i. working together towards a common goal
j. a condition in which a person cannot function in the real world
k. your total surroundings
l. the ability to stand up for yourself and express your feelings in a nonthreatening way
m. giving up something in order to reach an agreement
n. a condition in which fear blocks a person's ability to function normally
o. an unreasonable need to behave in a certain way

VOCABULARY